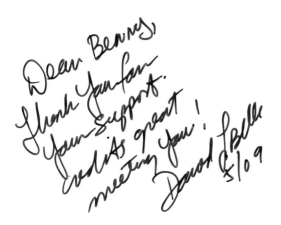

Dear Benny,
Thank you for
your support.
And it's great
meeting you!
David LaBelle
5/09

I don't want to know all the technical stuff ...
I JUST WANT TO SHOOT PICTURES

THE 'TLC' APPROACH TO TAKING GREAT PHOTOGRAPHS AT ANY AGE

By David LaBelle

Published by LaBelle Press
ISBN 978-1-60725-645-8

Mr. McArthur, who was always fascinated by flight, watches jet trails from his yard just months before his death in 2007.

In memory of Mr. Mac

This book is dedicated to the late Denning McArthur, "Mr. Mac" – my photography teacher, mentor, lifelong friend and so much more. Even with his failing eyes, he saw things others did not see.

Thank you for your compassionate spirit and for helping direct my life at such a crucial time. You gave so much to so many.

We miss you every day ...

Table of Contents

Chapter 4: Composition

- ✦ Get close and fill the frame
- ✦ Angle is everything
- ✦ Backgrounds
- ✦ Foregrounds
- ✦ Using picture space
- ✦ Pictures from the back
- ✦ Scale and contrast
- ✦ Showing cause and effect

Chapter 5: Other stuff you might want to know

- ✦ ASA and ISO
- ✦ Raw, JPEGs and TIFFs — digital files
- ✦ White balance settings
- ✦ Avoiding camera shake

Introduction

How many cubic centimeters does your car engine have? Or what's the number of pixels on your TV screen?

You say you don't know, and, frankly, *you don't care.*

Good!

Neither do I.

Most of us don't care how a car's motor is assembled or how many cubic centimeters its engine has. We care that it starts when we turn the ignition and that it can pass that monster semi when we tromp on the gas. Similarly, most of us are not interested in knowing the technical details of photography like f/stops, shutter speeds and megapixels. We just want to take better pictures and have fun doing it!

If you are one of these people, this book is for you.

After teaching photography for nearly 40 years, I have noticed a few common mistakes that, if corrected, would have turned average pictures into prize winners. By applying just a few of these simple techniques, you can begin shooting better pictures today.

Photography has never been easier … or more complicated. With photographic technology continually changing (faster, better films; automatic flashes, and digital cameras), this wildly popular hobby can seem overwhelming. But fear not, the core principles, the essentials of taking good pictures – timing, light and composition – never change.

So what are the real basics, those fundamental building blocks you need to begin shooting better pictures and enjoying photography more?

In the pages ahead, you'll find some time-tested tips guaranteed to have you shooting better pictures and having more fun with it.

But first, let's begin with the question I get asked most often:

What kind of camera should I buy? …

✳ Tip ✳

Keep it simple

The fewer bells and whistles a camera has, the easier it will be to use. Too many options can frustrate and discourage. As you grow in your understanding of photography, you may wish to step up to single-lens reflex (SLR) models that allow you to add lenses, rapid-fire settings and such. Many of these even have zoom lenses and built-in flashes. They vary in price from around $100 to $500 or more.

Chapter 1:

What kind of camera should I buy?

The type or brand of camera you use is not nearly as important as how you use it. After all, how to properly use any tool – whether a camera or a chainsaw – is the difference between an artist and an accident. Some of the greatest pictures ever taken have been made by amateurs with simple point-and-shoot cameras.

It is important to remember, regardless of how fancy it might look, that a camera is just a *tool* – a box that gathers light – and it is not nearly as important as the curiosity of the person carrying it.

I bought a digital videocamera recently, and after no less than six hours of reading the manual (a small version of the Los Angeles phonebook), I am still trying to figure it out. I have already missed important moments in my children's lives, because I can't operate the overly complex machine cluttered with features I will never use. Let's hope I figure it out before the kids get into college.

For every gizmo, there is a learning curve, and one more distraction to detract from capturing those special moments. Sometimes I mutter under my breath, "give me the old Kodak Instamatic."

Remember: *Good people, not good cameras, take good pictures!*

More than once I have had someone say, "Wow, that is a nice camera. I bet it takes good pictures."

I am reminded of a story I heard about a photographer sent to take pictures of a chef for a publication. Seeing the equipment, the subject said, "That is an expensive-looking camera. It must take great pictures." Annoyed by the insinuation, the photographer replied, "Yes, and those are nice pans. They must make great food."

When it comes to taking memorable pictures, *you* are the most important tool, *not the camera*; you are the artist, the master. You decide what's in your frame and when to press the shutter button. The camera will never be invented that has your heart, your instincts or your unique perspective.

Using a cell phone with a built-in digital camera, David Stephenson snaps a picture in his rearview mirror of his daughter, Tori, trying on her Mickey Mouse ears while driving in Southern California.

Patricia, a student in a photography and environmental workshop in Wilkinsburg, Pennsylvania, joyfully prepares to shoot one of her assignments.

Look for a camera that fits what you do – no more!

An automatic (disposable) camera that sets everything for you, even the flash, can be purchased for less than $10.

Don't get talked into buying ANYTHING that does more than you need or will use. Spending extra money on a bigger, more-expensive-looking camera with a bunch of bells and whistles is a waste and will frustrate, if not extinguish, the creative spirit. Besides, with the hundreds of dollars you save you'll be able to take a trip to shoot pictures.

If you are content with a camera that makes clean, crisp pictures, with a file size large enough to make 8-by-10-inch prints, and you don't care about changing lenses, then a simple point-and-shoot will do the job just fine. Many of these even have zoom lenses and built-in flashes.

✳ Tip ✳	✳ Caution ✳
Optional flash	**Shutter delay**
Be sure the camera you buy allows you to turn the flash off when you do not want to use it. Flash, like insurance, is only good when you need it.	Avoid cameras with a long delay from the time you press the shutter button until the camera fires. Otherwise, you will miss too many moments. It is the single biggest complaint I hear from photographers.

As you grow in your understanding of photography, you may wish to step up to a deluxe model with special features, but in the beginning, forget the camera and concentrate on the TLC of photography:

Timing, Light and Composition!

Chapter 2:
Timing

Great light is seductive, interesting composition is compelling, but I'll take a great moment above all the rest. A split second can be the difference between a great moment and a dull, non-moment. As in love and comedy, *timing is everything!*

After being warned not to forget his vows, Joey laughs as Danielle forgets hers and has to look at what she wrote. Staying focused on the threesome, I was able to make the picture.

Roses in hand, Nina waits for her boyfriend to arrive on a flight in Denver.

Anticipate

Have you ever noticed how some people seem luckier than others? You know, they bought the right house at the right price and it doubled in value, or they ran into the right person at the right time and advanced their career. Well, shooting picture moments is a little like that – it's a lot of luck or, as the saying goes, a lot of preparation meeting opportunity. With photography, magical life intersections occur where time and place meet in fleeting moments. If we're lucky, we can catch these once-in-a-lifetime happenings.

Knowing the players in any drama – be it a baseball game, political contest, reunion or wildlife shoot – and then anticipating where meaningful moments might happen greatly increases your odds of capturing memorable pictures. For example, before the last out of a close baseball game, ask yourself, *"Where should I be to get the best reaction?"* According to baseball tradition, players on the bench and on the field likely will rush the pitcher's mound for a celebration. This happens quickly, so being in the right position is important.

Having a camera handy is a first step. Some events happen in a split second, and there are no do-overs. Great photographs that live forever in books, albums and in our memories are usually pictures that tell stories. The light may be harsh or the composition cluttered, but if you capture that moment that tells a story, the rest is forgiven. In my book, content is king!

13

Under the heading of "you don't see that every day," I was able to fire off two quick frames from my van of a stuffed Grizzly riding in the back of a moving pickup. Yes, the picture could have been better if I had not been driving, but having a camera at hand allowed me to record the unusual sight. I tried turning around in traffic to get another picture and learn where the bruin was headed, but I could never catch up. My guess was that he was somebody's Christmas present.

Be prepared for the **unexpected**

Keeping a camera handy, with fresh batteries and film or a flash card loaded, is another way to increase your odds of capturing fleeting moments. When people learn I am a photographer, they often tell me stories of amazing or beautiful events they witnessed. And usually, after a long sigh, they bemoan, "If I had only had my camera with me."

Keeping a camera handy – especially in the car – allows you to capture unposed pictures of your children being children.

14

Be patient

Patience is another important tool. Often you will need to sit quietly, motionless, like a cat by a gopher hole, waiting for the picture you imagine to appear. If you are photographing wildlife, put your camera on a tripod. As you wait for that fox to come out of his den, that bird to feed its babies or that person to walk into that dramatic shaft of light, it will help keep the camera still and your arms and legs from cramping.

I found this fox den and could tell by the churned up earth and bones in front that it was being used. I waited about six hours before this little fellow finally popped out.

Using a fast shutter speed helped capture this picture of Junior, the youngest player on his Little League team, taking a mighty cut.

Stop action

There are times when you want to stop or freeze the action. One strength of still photography over moving pictures is that it allows you to study the details of a moment that happened in a fraction of a second. If your camera allows you to change shutter speeds, set your dial to 1/250th of a second or higher to freeze action. But even if you are using a point-and-shoot with a fixed shutter speed, you can still stop action just by timing the moment you press the shutter button – especially if the subject is coming toward you.

A fast shutter freezes a leaping pooch at a canine competition.

Create **motion**

If you want the opposite of freezing action, two simple techniques will help you create a feeling or sensation of motion in your pictures. The first is called *panning*. With panning, you press the shutter button while trying to move the camera at the same speed as your subject. The second way to introduce movement is to hold the camera still and allow a moving subject to blur through your frame. Both techniques require a little practice and experimentation, but expect to be surprised with some remarkable results.

By moving your camera at the same speed as your subject while pressing the shutter, you can create the feeling of motion, as with this picture of a rider at Keeneland Race Course in Lexington, Kentucky. If you have a camera that allows you to change the shutter speeds, try experimenting with slow shutter speeds like 1/15th or 1/30th of a second.

BAD is good!

Probably the three best things you can do to shoot better moments is to remember that *BAD – Before, After* and *During* an event or happening – is good. So often, it's before the event begins or after it ends that the best (the unrehearsed or candid) moments occur. And it is usually before we have picked up our cameras or after we have put them away.

As Kim Hughes becomes Kim O'Connor, she and her husband, Sean, share some sweet, unscripted moments.

Arriving early before a big event can produce wonderful candid moments, like this picture of Luke getting decked out for a religious ceremony.

Chapter 3:
LIGHT

Light is the river all photographers drink from, whether beginner or pro. Without it, there is neither life nor photography.

Learning to see light – especially dramatic light – is one of the joyful keys to shooting great pictures.

The color, intensity, direction and overall quality of light in our lives affects our moods and shapes the way we see and feel about everything: products, people, even the kind of day we have. The marketing and advertising worlds learned this early and are keenly aware of how light can set a mood for consumers to dig deep into their pockets. Consider how a warm shaft of golden light on a cold, rainy afternoon can brighten our mood or lift sagging spirits. Next time you find yourself emotionally drawn to a commercial or advertisement, or even a scene in a movie, take notice of the light. Chances are it is warm, yellow morning light or soft, diffused light or sharp rim or backlight.

What it probably won't be is flat, colorless (non-contrasty) light or sunlight from high noon. That is, unless you are watching reruns of *The Good, the Bad, and the Ugly*.

To help you become more familiar with light, we introduce the Light Family: a big brood with lots of brothers and sisters, each with distinct personalities and talents. The Light Ladies are all quality, while the Light Boys are about direction. In this chapter, you also will meet their cousins, the Flashes. Just as brothers or sisters often share family traits but remain individuals with unique personalities, light – though originating from one great source – has varying qualities and personalities, too.

Children of Light can be harsh, sharp, direct, soft, warm, cold or even moody – just like us.

Each member of the Light Family can influence your pictures greatly. In summary, the type or direction of light can create different moods in your pictures.

THE LIGHT BROTHERS

To help you better remember some important characteristics of light, let's meet the **Light Brothers**. These boys are all about direction of light. There is **Front**, **Back**, **Low**, **Top**, **Side** and **Reflected Light**. (And just for the record, these boys are indeed the brightest bulbs in the box.) As different as children of the same father can be, each brings something unique, something special to your pictures. In time, you will learn to recognize their differences

Late afternoon front light breaks through a storm-clouded sky illuminating an old barn near the Kentucky-Tennesee state line. You can tell the direction of the light by the shadows it creates.

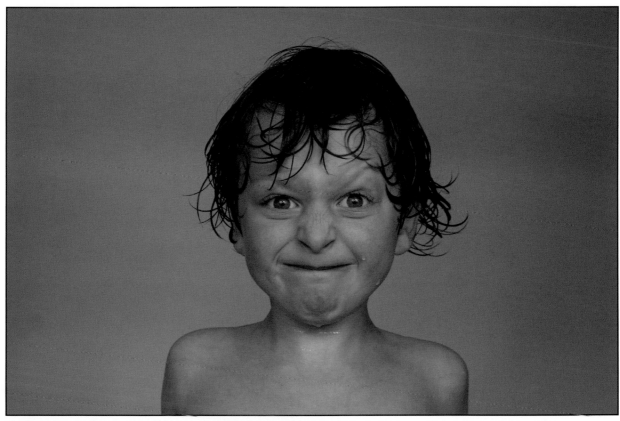

In this indoor picture of my son, Tucker, a 100-watt household bulb in the ceiling is the primary light source, an example of light coming from the front and above.

 Front light

First, let's meet **Front Light**. Front Light doesn't like wrinkles. He is often referred to as glamour light, because models adore him. He offers pretty much one-dimensional illumination that is less concerned with shape or depth and dimension than his brothers. Front light is what you see when the sun is at your back, shining into the face of your subject.

You can create this type of light just by taking the shade off a household lamp and holding it in front of your subject. In this indoor picture, the light is coming from above and front.

Top light

The most popular of all the Light Brothers, **Top Light** usually shows up around noon, creating deep, dark shadows beneath hats and even in eye sockets. Some people like to add flash when shooting with Top Light, to help lighten or "open" shadows.

When **Front Light** comes from above and creates small shadows beneath the nose, this is called **Top Front Light**. Notice how a single, diffused light source from front and above helps reveal Katherine's natural beauty.

Low light

Much the opposite of his flattering big brother, Top Light, **Low Light** makes most of his appearances on stage, near campfires or around Halloween. Though the least famous of the Light Brothers, he does have his days in the sun. When pictures call for haunting or "monster" lighting, Low Light is often the first called. He casts long shadows upward, creating a dramatic, mysterious look. Like most of the Light Brothers, Low Light can come to your pictures in a variety of sources: sunlight, strobe light, spotlight or even candlelight, to name a few. But for mysterious-looking, attention-getting results, he prefers flashlight.

Notice how different sweet Katherine looks when the quality and direction of the light changes.

A setting sun brings a strong **Side Light**, which creates shadows that reveal tracks and show the texture of the landscape in New Mexico's White Sands National Monument.

Side light

Side Light comes by his name naturally, because he approaches subjects from the side. He creates shadows that help show texture and shape in your pictures. Photographers often call on him to reveal the shape of a face or fabric detail or to create a sculpted look in portraits.

Side Light from a rising sun strikes Valentin's face en route to becoming a U.S. citizen.

Reflected light

Have you ever walked down the street and your face suddenly lights up (literally) and you find yourself bathed in a golden light? Chances are you just met **Reflected Light** bouncing the sun's rays off a wall, a window or a large pane of glass. So magical is Reflected Light, he makes you want to curl up on the sidewalk like a cat and bask in his golden warmth. And even though he is often seen bouncing off walls, Reflected Light is, as his name suggests, quiet and reflective. Softer than his brother, Direct Light, Reflected Light catches the light of a greater source and gently shares it. He can be found almost anywhere: on rock walls, white-sand beaches or even concrete walkways. Like a magic genie, he can be summoned any time you need a little "light pick-me-up" or to help fill in those high-noon shadows. All you need is an object that will reflect light: a piece of aluminum foil, a white sheet, a piece of white cardboard or one of those inexpensive, shiny dashboard protectors.

If you do a lot of portraits, you might consider purchasing a reflector kit that has white, gold or silver surfaces.

Ryan uses an easy-to-find dashboard protector to catch the sunlight and reflect it onto Brooke's face. Notice how the reflected light brightens the shadows.

Above: Backlight creates a rim of light around a young buck with velvet antlers. The light shows the shape of the deer as well as every whisker, which I didn't realize deer had. Maybe it's a guy thing?

Left: The light coming from behind Henry's head as he studies a lizard creates an angelic rim of light, evoking a hopeful feeling. Light reflecting from the wooden beam also helps to illuminate his face. Some of the best photos happen when more than one of the Light Brothers work together to give you just the right touch.

Backlight

The next of the Light brothers is **Backlight**. Not as direct or as harsh as his brothers, Backlight is more quiet and poetic. He looks into the camera from behind subjects, revealing their shapes and often creating a beautiful, angelic rim of light that helps separate them from their backgrounds. Backlight is a good example of NOT buying into the old concept that you should always have the sun at your back when shooting pictures.

When photographing plants or foliage, Backlight can also be a great help to show shapes.

Light coming from behind or through your subject helps define shape, as seen with this eucalyptus tree, above, and this autumn leaf, left. **Backlight** coming through the leaf adds brilliance to the color, which helps it stand out against the darker background.

A late afternoon sun bathes Anna in golden light as she rides home on a train.

THE LIGHT SISTERS

Now, meet the **Light Sisters**. Not to be outdone by their illuminating brothers, these "light-on-their-feet" ladies are all about quality and character of light, and about setting a mood. First, meet **Warm Light**. Everybody wants to be around her. She makes us feel good and hopeful about life and is in constant demand, especially in advertising circles. When marketing gurus want to sell you on a concept, they often call on warm, golden light to connect your eye, heart and wallet.

Cold light

Next, comes **Cold Light**. The opposite of her sister, she doesn't warm up to people as quickly. Blues, grays, dark greens and blacks are her favorite colors. And often she is dramatic, preferring to operate in the cold, blue shadows rather than the warm yellow or orange sunlight.

Overcast skies and billowing storm clouds create a cold, monochromatic feel to this California hilltop scene. **Cold Light** makes you want to wrap your hands around a warm cup of coffee or hot chocolate.

Soft light

Now, let me introduce you to **Soft Light**. She is a poet, an artist and a master at making older folks look younger and melting wrinkles. With soft light, the world is not so harsh. She gently spreads a delicate veil, diffusing the light and softening sharp shadows. Her softness comes as she passes through clouds, window shades, pieces of cloth or other light-colored fabrics.

Both this red-tailed hawk and this barn owl were photographed beneath a white canvas tarp with light coming through from above.

Hard light

The third sister is **Hard Light**, the oldest and most direct in the Light Family and the one seen most often. No nonsense, she is pointed and doesn't care whether you like her or not. She is confident and can be found almost anywhere photographs are made. You can spot her by the sharp shadows she creates. She can be harsh and tough to deal with at times. Perhaps that is why some photographers avoid her and live in places like Seattle or Pittsburgh, where she is kept in check by the more even, softer, gray skies. If faces are important, it is often wise to use a little fill flash or a reflector to lighten the harsh shadows she creates. You can find hard light just about anywhere: spotlights, stage lights or bright, sunny days.

A sharp, hard light warms Tucker's feet as he swings in a backyard hammock. On clear, crisp days – usually found in the winter or fall – hard light abounds because of fewer clouds and less atmospheric haze to soften its reach.

Above: Afternoon shadows of those waiting in line at a Kentucky carnival.
Right: Using the tall shadows of this frontyard plant in Denver as the dominant portion of the picture creates a more beautiful and visualy interesting photo than focusing just on the plant.

Shadows

We talked about "opening up" or "filling" shadows, but lest they get maligned, shadows can be one of a photographer's best friends.

Without them, life and light would be dull and flat. Shadows – especially long ones created by an early morning or late afternoon sun – add dimension, crispness, contrast, shape and drama to our pictures. They also can make for some fun images.

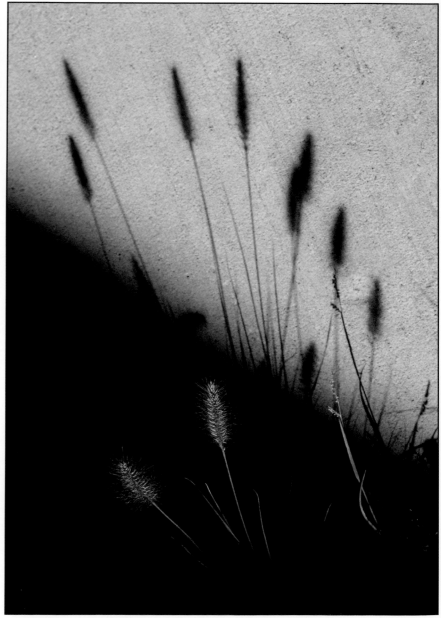

Finding
the light

One way to take advantage of beautiful or striking light is to find it first, then bring subjects to it or wait for them to come to the light on their own. The picture above was shot first. I noticed a shaft of light streaming in from the ceiling and waited for the young lady to pass through it. The dramatic light is the difference between an average picture and a compelling one.

Creating cool silhouettes

The secret to clean, easy-to-read silhouettes is making sure you have uncluttered backgrounds where tones do not merge or blend together. When you expose for the light behind your subject, the shadowy shape of your subject is defined, as with these graveyard crosses in New Mexico and this hawk in Georgia.

Shooting into the light

When I began shooting pictures as a child, I was told, "keep the sun at your back and don't shoot into the light." I learned later that advice, however well-meaning, was extremely limiting.

Shooting into the light can give your pictures shape, depth and a mood not achieved with the sun at your back. It is true – and perhaps that was at the core of the advice – that strong light coming directly into your lens can cause flaring, not to mention seriously damaging your eyes if you stare into a bright sun. That said, daring to shoot into the light can offer beautiful and interesting results.

Another problem often occurs when you try to take pictures of people in the shade while you are standing in the sun. You have probably noticed your pictures lacked contrast and appeared washed out when you did this.

If you are able, try getting into the shade with your subject to make your pictures. I think you will see a world of difference.

* Tip *

Shooting pictures in shade can offer a soft, even light void of sharp and contrasty shadows. This will help reduce the overall flare and washed-out feeling that happens if you stand in sunlight while making pictures of subjects in the shade.

* Tip *

One way to avoid lens flare is to use a hat to shade the lens and block the sun's direct rays from hitting the lens.

Ryan holds his hat at an angle that blocks the sunlight from his lens while shooting a picture of his bride.

Light & color

When it comes to light and color, time of year and time of day are everything. No doubt you have noticed how light and color differ by the season and by the hour. In winter, for instance, the blues are richer and the light sharper, less-diffused, and even the clouds are shaped differently. It has long been understood that the best light and the richest color are often found 30 minutes before and after sunrise and sunset. Below are four images of the Colorado State Capitol in Denver taken at different times of day.

5 a.m.

6 a.m.

Noon

5:30 p.m.

By steadying the camera on a tripod and using a slow shutter speed of 3 or 4 seconds, we allow the lights of the Ferris wheel to twirl and create motion.

A homeless person sits alone in a Pittsburgh park, illuminated only by the street lamps. Using a flash would have totally changed the mood.

Shooting in low light or **after sunset**

Just because you are indoors, with relatively little light, or the sun has already slipped below the horizon doesn't mean you need flash to shoot great pictures. As a matter of fact, using the existing light will produce far more natural-looking photos. But to take good pictures in low light, you will need to take one of two steps: Change your ISO dial to something higher, say 400 or above. Or use a slow shutter speed of something likely below 1/2 of a second. When using slow shutter speeds, you must hold your camera still. Brace it on something firm, like a parked car, wall or tripod. With a tripod you can shoot long exposures and get wonderful results with little light.

You might have to figure out how to temporarily disable or turn your flash off to shoot long exposures. If your flash is built in to your camera, try covering it with a piece of black tape or cardboard. Above all, experiment!

MEET the FLASHES

Finally, we meet **The Flashes**: **Direct**, **Bounce** and **Fill**. An illuminating and versatile trio, the Flashes can help your camera see subjects in the dark; add contrast and brighten color on dull, overcast days; fill in harsh shadows on bright sunny days; and even freeze motion. But it has been my experience that most people fear the Flashes and are not quite sure how to handle them. Once you spend a little time with them, you will learn how much help they can be to your pictures.

And when the Flashes get a little harsh, as can be the case with Direct Flash, you can always soften them by diffusing them – covering them with a white sheet of plastic, cloth or even paper.

Sometimes called strobes, most cameras these days come with built-in and "pop-up" flashes. Other flashes, called external flashes, can be attached by a synch cord or "hot shoe."

Using flash allows us to both illuminate subjects and freeze motion, as in this picture of Brenna trick-or-treating on Halloween night.

Flash on a dark, gray day adds color and contrast to a joyful Henry at the beach.

✳ Tip ✳

A variety of diffusers (equipment to soften the light) can be found to fit over pop-up flashes. The inexpensive yet effective one at left was created by Gary Fong.

Here is Direct Flash doing his thing – illuminating – so we can see Henry and his fish and study picture details.

Direct flash

This family of three is led by the father of all flashes, **Direct Flash**, who got his name because he doesn't mince words – or light. He comes straight at you, providing a no-nonsense, in-your-face illumination. And though he doesn't mean to, he can be pretty harsh at times. That said, when it comes to the camera seeing what's happening in a dark situation, nobody does it better than Direct Flash. He is the "quick draw" of light, able to catch jumping cats or flying owls in the night, all the while revealing important details. By far the most popular of the flashes, Direct Flash – once kept separate from the camera body – is built in to most cameras these days.

✳ Tip ✳

Since Direct Flash likes to bring his shadow along, it's a good idea to pose your subjects away from walls when photographing them.

Fill flash

"Even in the day?" my friend Nan asked about using her flash.

"Yes, even in the day," I answered.

On bright, sunny days, with shadows more plentiful than fish, **Fill Flash** lights up those shadowy faces. When your subjects are backlighted or in shadow, Fill Flash is a nice cosmetic touch to lighten up those beautiful faces. In his purest form, Fill Flash is adding a little less light (flash) than the existing light. If you have a camera that allows you to reduce the amount of flash output, cutting back the flash by one or two stops will give you the best results for filling in those shadows. If you cannot adjust your flash, just take a step or two back to achieve a similar effect.

Fill Flash is asked to do his magic and open those shadows a little so we can see Henry and Tucker at Dodger Stadium in Los Angeles.

Bounce flash

Whether he is bouncing his light off the ceiling, a wall or a white card, **Bounce Flash** can be your best friend – especially at parties or meetings held in fluorescent-lit rooms with low ceilings. When his illuminating burst of light explodes, it strikes surfaces – ceilings, walls, a white card – and bounces its light back, falling ever so gently on your subjects, creating a much softer feel. Using a bounce light is also a good way to eliminate unwanted shadows that often show up behind your subjects if they are near walls. Aiming your strobe/flash up and bouncing the light off of the ceiling is easy to do and produces a softer, more flattering look to your pictures – especially in a fluorescent room.

Bouncing the light off the ceiling and from a pop-up card that bounces the light of the flash, Tucker and I do an after-bath self-portrait.

Using the on-camera pop-up flash does illuminate Mary, but the light is sharp, contrasty and unflattering, not doing her pretty face justice.

Notice how much softer and more pleasant the light is here on Mary, my Christian sister.

Chapter 4:
COMPOSITION

The historic Duquesne Incline with a view of Pittsburgh's Golden Triangle.

Think of your viewfinder as an artist's canvas. After all, what you choose to include in your frame and the moment you choose to press the shutter has everything to do with your individuality and your artistic impression. To me, composition – how things are arranged in your viewfinder – is a stage you build while waiting for the performance to begin.

Composition has no rules, except those subjective ones that some people try to impose on others. Have fun and experiment. The picture police won't come confiscate your photos.

No two people see life exactly alike. Your photo composition speaks volumes about what you think is interesting or important and how you see the world.

When you compose, try to use all four corners of your frame. Remember, the camera sees everything.

A bicyclist peforms at the Kentucky State Fair in Louisville.

A semi-candid portrait of Tucker, shot by his mother.

Get close

Each year I judge thousands of photographs that could have been improved greatly just by getting closer and filling the frame.

I remember a student who came rushing to class nearly out of breath, excitedly telling me about this beautiful picture she had made of a deer in a meadow. "Let's see it," I said, wanting to share in her accomplishment. When she finally calmed down enough to show me the picture, I was dumbfounded.

I couldn't find the deer anywhere. Seeing my bewildered expression, she pointed to a small brown speck, no bigger than a pinhead. "There, right there he is."

You are not always going to have time to get closer and fill the frame as precisely as you would like. But when you do have time, practicing compositional craftsmanship will make your pictures better, and those viewing them won't have to guess what they are supposed to look at.

✳ Tip ✳

When photographing children and pets, try getting on their level and photographing them in their environment, as with Riley, above. Often when we change our angle, we not only clean up our backgrounds, we also change the feeling of the picture, as with this cow in Denver.

ANGLE

"Look up, look down, look all around." Those words to a song I remember as a kid are good advice for any photographer. After all, things look quite different from above than they do from below. You can make subjects look powerful or vulnerable, depending on the angle you choose to photograph from.

is everything

Jake poses for a picture, unsuspecting of the background.

Those busy **backgrounds**

Oh, those naughty backgrounds!

Surely they are responsible for many disappointed faces as excited eyes search digital screens or newly processed prints, only to find attention-stealing poles and wires cluttering their prized pictures. Consider the millions of "average" photos shot each year that might have been "great" if we had only noticed those blossoming begonias growing from grandma's blue hair. Or that tree branch sprouting from Uncle Arthur's bald head as if he were wearing a set of jackalope antlers. Backgrounds can make or break pictures. They can be helpful or harmful, supporting actors or show-stealing pests.

Bad, noisy backgrounds are mischievous children, trying to steal attention from your subjects and disrupt your careful compositions with ugly mergers. Image hogs, they sometimes go so far as to mock your subjects, placing antlers or rabbit ears on unsuspecting folks. They slip into your pictures unnoticed – a tree branch here, an electrical wire there. Because we are so busy concentrating on our main subject, we don't see them ... until it's too late.

Good backgrounds, on the other hand, accept their place in pictures and quietly go about their work of visually seasoning your photos with supporting, non-competing shapes and colors. Great mood-setters, these backgrounds, like soft music, gracefully complement your pictures with subtle lines or tones that help viewers feel the tempo of your image, much the way music leads us to a love scene.

Remember, you are the parent of your pictures — the artist, the composer, the director. You decide what's in your viewfinder and when to press the shutter. But be advised, the camera might see things you don't.

Bad backgrounds are not really evil. They are just mischievous, undisciplined pranksters crying for attention. Under a watchful eye and with a little care, they can actually be quite helpful. Spend a little time with them, appreciate them, direct them, maybe even play a game of hide-and-seek with them, and they will behave.

Look beyond your subjects and see what is happening behind them – in the background. Don't be too trusting and assume your backgrounds are behaving themselves. Remember, they are by nature children of mischief and they love to cause trouble.

You might even have to bend your knees or move a little to the left or right to organize them, but they will behave if you keep a firm eye.

Basically, you can move your subjects or move your camera.

The background in this picture of Steve, a veteran marching in a Fourth of July Parade, doesn't steal the attention from the main subject or create an ugly merger. Instead, the supporting background quietly helps provide additional information while adding depth to the photo.

Above: This musical-feeling picture, shot by my wife, Erin, is a great example of timing and a photograph with several layers of information, creating depth without ugly or confusing mergers.

Left: The picture of a sea lion frolicking in a Rhode Island aquarium is a lot more interesting with the silhouetted family in the foreground.

Our **foreground** friends

Foregrounds are our friends.

The opposite of their background cousins, foregrounds are to be seen first, as sort of picture-greeters or visual hosts. It's their job, and a noble one at that, to take us by the eyes and gently lead us through a photograph's layers of information. As table-setters for good composition, they also can be helpful devices to direct us to a photograph's main subject. By using color, shape and tone, foregrounds can be frames that hold our visual arrangements together while giving contrast and depth to our pictures. Like a mint on a pillow at an expensive hotel, strong foregrounds are accents that can add a touch of class to most pictures. Ideally, foregrounds and backgrounds should work together to convey information and create storytelling pictures.

As my dear photography teacher often said when teaching about composition, look for "something near, something far." Sage advice that still holds true.

When photographing breathtaking sunrises or sunsets, foregrounds are valuable tools, providing contrast, dimension and framing.

Using picture space

There is a time to get close and see details and a time to back up and include more environment in our pictures. The space we use in our photos not occupied by our subject is called negative space. How much space to include in a composition is an individual choice and not a matter of right or wrong.

A couple of suggestions about using space in our pictures: Space and tone can create mood. For instance, a picture with a small subject and a lot of negative space can feel lonely. Also, when you use more negative space in front of your subject than behind him, you create an energy and the sensation of motion, as though your subject has somewhere to go and is on the way to getting there. If you use more space behind him, it is as though he has been somewhere. But when your subject is dead center in the frame, he is frozen, suspended. Generally, it's believed that pictures where subjects are positioned in one of the imaginary intersections where the frame is divided into thirds, called the Golden Mean or Rule of Thirds, are more alive and interesting. That said, sometimes having the subject or subjects in the middle of the frame is more compelling, depending on the subject. My advice is don't get locked into any set of compositional rules.

Choose how to use your picture space to achieve the feel you want in your pictures.

Here are two pictures of a Colorado rancher named Paul. In the top frame, Paul is centered. By getting just a little higher and using Paul in the right third of the frame, the picture becomes a little more active and alive, and we also take better advantage of the beautiful mountain scenery.

Rule of thirds
It is generally thought that pictures have more tension or energy and are more interesting when subjects are arranged in one these four imaginary intersections, as opposed to centering your subjects.

Pictures from **the back**

Top: Buddies Ryan and Henry sit by a creek in Colorado.
Above: Children dressed for Halloween take a stroll on a California hillside in this photo taken by my wife, Erin.

Every time I hear some well-meaning teacher scold students for shooting subjects from the back, I want to take him by the ears and lead him through a historical photo archive. Some of my favorite pictures, and some of the greatest historical images ever made, were shot from the back: George Tames' famous image of JFK working at his desk; Nat Fein's 1948 Pulitzer-Prize winning photo titled "The Babe Bows Out," showing Babe Ruth waving goodbye at Yankee stadium; W. Eugene Smith's engaging photograph of his children titled "The Walk to Paradise Garden" – all shot with the subjects facing away from the camera. And why not? Our posture often reveals a lot about us. Besides, not facing somebody gives the viewer room to imagine and dream, and we can project and see ourselves or others in the picture more easily.

More than once, I have seen a wonderful moment happening and then somebody yells, "turn around so we can see your faces." The moment is gone. Arghhh! Don't buy into it. If the picture is more interesting from the back – and it often is – shoot it without apology.

Without the two human figures, we wouldn't have a size reference for this beached humpback whale.

Scale & **contrast**

How big is a fence lizard? We can say, "Well, about 6 inches." But what does that mean? The best way to understand most things – especially when talking size – is to measure them against something common, something most know. We say golf-ball size hail, or as big as an elephant. With photography, scale – which shows size and contrast, which has to do with tones or appearances – is an important visual communication tool.

Sometimes, fashion photographers pose models in greasy junkyards or ghetto backdrops for the sake of extreme contrast – sort of a beauty-and-beast look. By placing one object near another, we get a better understanding of size differences. Unlike words, the understanding is immediate.

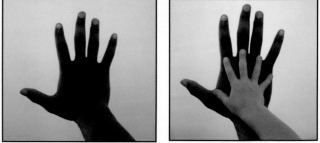

Malachi is a football player with large hands.

Left: Henry reacts to seeing a baby robin move in its nest. **Below:** A fascinated Ryan studies the dead body of a small snake.

Pictures that show
cause & effect

Some of my favorite pictures are those that can stand alone and tell a story with few words.

One of my greatest influences, the painter Norman Rockwell, was a master at storytelling using cause and effect. Sometimes an action alone is interesting, but when you capture both the action and the reaction, your pictures will become more complete – more storytelling.

Molly is amused when her daughter pretends to talk on the phone, though nobody is on the other end.

Chapter 5:
OTHER STUFF YOU MIGHT WANT TO KNOW

ASA and ISO: Sensitivity twins

ASA and ISO. What in the cat hair are these?

As with any new subject, some terms are worth learning. But don't get bogged down in confusing language that will kill your spirit of photo adventure. You will find camera junkies who use terms I don't understand. Usually these folks talk more than they shoot. Most good photographers I know speak more about their subjects than about their gear.

That said, a few basic terms are useful, including ISO and ASA. Twins, they refer to the same thing: to the speed or the light sensitivity of a film, or with digital photography, the sensor sensitivity. In theory, they are the same thing. ASA (American Standards Association), an older term not often used these days, refers to the film speed rating in the United States. ISO is the same thing (International Standards Organization) and has all but replaced ASA.

The higher the ISO/ASA, the more sensitive your film is to light (or sensor, if using digital photography).

During the golden era of photography in the early 1900s, film speeds were slow, most about ASA 25 to 100. Nowadays, it is nothing to use a film or "sensor speed" of 1600 or above. A "fast" film speed of ISO 400 is four times more sensitive to light than a speed of 100. Higher ISO settings allow you to shoot pictures in lower or darker situations with faster shutter speeds, but with less range of tonal quality. Like our eyes, which struggle to see detail in dark scenes, low ISO settings, like 100, are not sensitive enough to see details in low light. But high ISO settings, say 400 and above, allow the camera to record in low light, like the eyes of an owl or nocturnal animal. Generally speaking, the higher the ISO, the less quality or information the camera is able to record. With digital, this grainy effect is called "noise."

Basically, it is a trade-off. The higher the ISO, the faster shutter speeds can be used and/or wider apertures, but the image quality will suffer accordingly. Decide which is more important: image file quality or getting a picture of a moment that might not look like an Ansel Adams print, but conveys the joyful happening.

I shoot most landscape pictures in the Raw mode, which gives me a higher quality file in the event that I want to make larger prints.

Should I shoot in **Raw, TIFF** or **JPEG**?

And what does that all mean, anyway? Good question. Similar to buying a camera, you need to ask what you want to do with your pictures. If just shooting snapshots to put in an album, file size is not so important. But if you are a stickler for quality and might want to make large prints or sell your images for use in a book or magazine, file size can be critical.

In brief, JPEG files, especially small ones, say 2 megs or less, do not contain as much information in the file as say a large JPEG or a TIFF file. Most cameras allow you choices even in the file sizes of the JPEGS. I shoot in large JPEG file mode most often.

Then there is Raw: a favorite mode because it allows you to correct exposure mistakes or even change white balance settings after the fact. Sort of seems like cheating. But Raw takes longer for your camera to write (record the information on the sensor) and requires more space on your flash card. While you can take 500 or so images on a 1Mg flash card with a medium JPEG setting, you might be able to shoot only 50 or so in Raw.

If this interests you, go online and read discussions about the differences. Many technical books are also available. I shoot Raw mostly when I am doing landscapes in case I want to make exhibition prints later.

What is **white balance**?
Why is it important?

If you are shooting with a digital camera, white balance settings are important.

Imagine looking at a beautiful blue sky with orange lenses in your glass frames. That's what your camera does if your white balance setting is incorrect. It renders an incorrect color. Without going into too much detail, white balance is based on a color temperature scale. Colder or bluer temperatures are given higher numbers on the Kelvin rating scale, and warmer, redder temperatures get lower numbers.

What does this mean? Not too much if you have an "A" white balance setting. In AUTO, the camera looks at the scene and averages the color temperature and adjusts accordingly, kind of like those polaroid glasses that adjust to the changing light when you go inside or out. If you want to be more precise, you can likely adjust your settings for more accurate white balance readings. Your camera probably has settings like sunny, shady, fluorescent, tungsten or incandescent.

But for most of us, the AUTO white balance setting will do just fine.

Because I was moving in and out of different types of light, I set the white balance setting on Auto when I shot this picture of lambs being shaved and washed for showing at the Kentucky State Fair.

Avoiding camera **shake**

It is amazing how many pictures I see that look like they were shot during a California earthquake: blurred images of boyfriends and girlfriends, children, pets, even buildings that were holding perfectly still.

Unless you are actually shooting during an earthquake, or an exotic bird creeps up and gooses you from behind just as you take the picture – which has happened to me – then just the slightest bit of care to hold the camera steady will do wonders for your dizzy pictures. The old practice of holding your breath or timing your breathing, and not jabbing the shutter button as though it's an ant that has climbed on the dinner table, can do wonders to stabilize movement. And if you are the wiggly, nervous type, bracing yourself and the camera on a car or against a house or other stable object will do the trick. Finally, I suggest you invest in a tripod (a three-legged gizmo) or a monopod (a one-legged gizmo).

Tripods come in all sizes and prices. For a minimal amount, you can even find a table-top model for your camera bag or purse. These babies are worth their weight in gold when it comes to steadying your camera.

Above: Henry, above, casts a shadow as he puts a camera on a tripod.
Right: Callie steadies her hands on the corner while shooting a picture of her cat.

During a break in Photographic Society of America photo judging, David LaBelle snags a picture of himself and other judges, Carol Guzy and Tom Kennedy. Photo by Lynn Maniscalco.

Have fun! I can offer no better advice.

Don't let the things you don't know keep you from shooting the kinds of pictures you love to take. And please, please don't let the "rules" of photography discourage you from taking pictures the way you see and feel. "Rules" are for those who live in fear of making mistakes. And for those without imagination. Experiment!